D0577584

Vincent
VAN GOGH

Vincent
VAN GOGH

Gareth Stevens Publishing
A WORLD ALMANAC EDUCATION GROUP COMPANY

Please visit our web site at:
www.worldalmanaclibrary.com
For a free color catalog describing World Almanac®
Library's list of high-quality books and multimedia
programs, call 1-800-848-2928 (USA) or 1-800-387-3178
(Canada). World Almanac® Library's fax: (414) 332-3567.

Library of Congress Cataloging-in-Publication Data available upon request
from publisher. Fax (414) 336-0157 for the attention of the Publishing
Records Department.

ISBN 0-8368-5602-3 (lib. bdg.)
ISBN 0-8368-5607-4 (softcover)

This North American edition first published in 2004 by
World Almanac® Library
330 West Olive Street, Suite 100
Milwaukee, WI 53212 USA

This U.S. edition copyright © 2004 by World Almanac® Library.
Original edition copyright © 2004 McRae Books Srl.

The series "The Lives of the Artists"
was created and produced by McRae Books Srl
Borgo Santa Croce, 8 – Florence (Italy)
info@mcraebooks.com
Publishers: Anne McRae and Marco Nardi

Project Editor: Loredana Agosta
Art History consultant: Roberto Carvalho de Magalhães
Text: Andrea Bassil
Illustrations: Studio Stalio (Alessandro Cantucci,
Fabiano Fabbrucci, Andrea Morandi)
Graphic Design: Marco Nardi
Picture Research: Claire Andrews
Layout: Studio Yotto
World Almanac® Library editor: JoAnn Early Macken
World Almanac® Library art direction: Tammy Gruenewald

Acknowledgments
All efforts have been made to obtain and provide compensation for
the copyright to the photos and artworks in this book in accordance
with legal provisions. Persons who may nevertheless still have claims
are requested to contact the copyright owners.

t=top; tl=top left; tc=top center; tr=top right; c=center; cl=center left;
cr= center right; b=bottom; bl=bottom left; bc=bottom center;
br=bottom right

The publishers would like to thank the following archives who have
authorized the reproduction of the works in this book:
The Bridgeman Art Library, London/Farabola Foto, Milano: 3, 4, 6cr, 7tr,
9cr, 10b, 11br, 13b, 16b, 17br, 19t, 20c, 21t, 22tr, 22cl, 23t, 23b, 24cr, 24bl, 25t,
25cl, 25b, 26br, 27cl, 28l, 28r, 29r, 30b, 31t, 31br, 32b, 33t, 37bc, 38t, 38cl, 39,
40cl, 41t, 41b, 43, 45b; Foto Scala, Florence: cover, 32t, 36b, 37tr, 40b; Rue
des Archives, Paris: 8cr, 16cr, 33b; Photos12, Paris/Grazia Neri,Srl, Milan:
20bl, 26bl, 37bl; Corbis/Contrasto, Milano: Yves Forestier 11t, 14, 15cr,
Francis G. 29cl, 39bl, Charles O'Rear 7cl, Christie's Images 7b; Archivio
Electa, Milano: 9b, 27tr

The publishers would like to thank the following museums and
institutions who have authorized the reproduction of the works in this
book: Van Gogh Museum Foundation, Amsterdam: 5, 10tr, 11bl, 17cl, 18cr,
19bl, 21b, 30cl, 42bl; Collection Kröller-Müller Museum, Otterlo: 9t, 12b,
17t; ©Tate, London 2003: 45t; Photograph © 2003 Museum of Fine Arts,
Boston; Rijksmuseum, Amsterdam: 15b; Digital Image © 2003 The
Museum of Modern Art/Scala, Florence: 34–35; ©Francis Bacon, by SIAE
2003: 45tr; ©Edvard Munch, By SIAE 2003: 45bl; Statens Museum for
Kunst, Copenhagen ©Succession H. Matisse by SIAE 2003: 44

All rights reserved. No part of this book may be reproduced, stored
in a retrieval system, or transmitted in any form or by any means,
electronic, mechanical, photocopying, recording, or otherwise,
without the prior written permission of the copyright holder.

Printed in China

1 2 3 4 5 6 7 8 9 08 07 06 05 04

cover: *Self-Portrait*, **Musée d'Orsay, Paris**
above: *Wheat Field with Crows*, **Rijksmuseum Vincent van Gogh,**
     Amsterdam,
opposite: *The Courtesan (after Eisen)*, **Rijksmuseum Vincent van Gogh**
     Amsterdam
previous page: *Self-Portrait with a Bandaged Ear*, **Courtauld Institute**
     Galleries, London,

Table of Contents

Introduction

van Gogh's **NETHERLANDS**

Amsterdam
The Hague
Zevenbergen
Groot-Zundert / Nuenen

Vincent van Gogh's career only covered about ten years, but during this time, he produced more than eight hundred paintings and a huge number of drawings and sketches. He was virtually self-taught, and much of his learning, he would claim, was derived from a lifelong study of old masters. When his vocation to preach failed, he focused on developing his artistic talent with financial support and encouragement from his brother Theo. He may have been labeled a Postimpressionist, but the emotional torment expressed in his work led him to develop a highly individual style that is hard to categorize.

Vincent's Letters to Theo

Although Vincent felt isolated and rejected by society, he was a fantastic communicator. An insight into this troubled character's inner life has been gained from the wealth of letters he wrote and illustrated. He wrote nine hundred letters that are now well documented, and most are held by the van Gogh Museum in Amsterdam. Most of the letters were written to his brother and supporter Theo. Vincent and Theo were in continual communication. The letters are testament to Theo's unfailing faith in his brother's talent. On Theo's death in 1914, six months after Vincent's suicide, Theo's widow collected and published a number of the letters between the two brothers.

▲ *A letter written by Vincent to Theo in 1883 with* Man Pulling a Harrow.

▼ *The van Gogh Museum, designed by Gerrit Rietveld, opened in Amsterdam in 1973. Millions of people have now visited the museum.*

The van Gogh Museum

Vincent felt very indebted to his brother for his unfailing financial support and in return sent him numerous canvases. As an art dealer, Theo regarded this as an acceptable agreement. At the time, Vincent was almost completely unknown, so it was fortuitous that on Theo's death, the family did not distribute the paintings. These works formed the basis of the collection of the van Gogh Museum in Amsterdam.

The Great Auction Sales

Vincent sold very few paintings in his lifetime because he had an aversion to commercial popularity. Some of his works were sold by Père Tanguy in his shop. After his death, thanks to his family, his work received public acclaim, and its value has been rising ever since. In 1891, a mere 230 francs was paid for *Irises*. Nearly a hundred years later, in 1987, this painting was sold at auction for $53.9 million. By 1990, a record $82.5 million was paid for the portrait of Dr. Gachet by a Japanese businessman. Works by van Gogh sold for two of the top ten prices ever paid for paintings at auction.

▲ Self-Portrait *(1889). This portrait, showing Vincent without a beard, was painted for his mother the year before he died.*

◀ *Although few sold during his lifetime, van Gogh's paintings now sell for millions.*

▼ *The works of van Gogh have been sold in some of the most prestigious auction houses, such as Christie's.*

▶ Still Life: Vase with Fifteen Sunflowers *(1889), known as* Yasuda Sunflowers, *was bought by a Japanese insurance magnate for $39,921.*

Fakes Controversy

Since 1928, when it came to light that a German art dealer had produced a number of fakes, a great deal of controversy has surrounded the question of the authenticity of some of van Gogh's works. J.B. de la Faille first published a catalogue raisonné that revealed a number of these fakes. By 1970, as many as forty-nine paintings and drawings were established as fakes. Questions about the Yasuda *Sunflowers* have raged since 1997 when two researchers queried its status. Some perceive it as a poor copy of the work in the National Gallery in London. Vincent's correspondence gives accounts of two sunflower paintings with fourteen flowers. The question arises as to whether the three that now exist are all genuine. The authenticity of some paintings still remains under contention because the list exceeds the amount of work that Vincent could possibly have produced.

Early Life

The son of a Calvinist minister and an active, artistic mother, Vincent was born and raised in a small village in the Netherlands. The couple's firstborn son, also called Vincent, was born and died on March 30, curiously the same date Vincent was born. This history haunted him and made him question his identity. He developed a close bond with his younger brother Theo, who was to help and guide him through his life. The two communicated by letters, many of which Vincent illustrated.

▲ Vincent was raised in the flat Dutch landscape with its clear horizon lines, whirring windmills, and golden fields of corn.

Lonely Childhood

Although Vincent was the oldest of six children, he spent much of his time alone. He loved nature and often wandered alone in the countryside, watching birds and catching insects. Although he drew little at this time, his early fascination with landscape formed the basis for many of his later paintings. Vincent was not a good pupil. When he was sent to boarding school, he found it a sad, lonely time. Despite being intelligent, he did not do well academically. When he was fifteen, his father sent him out to work.

▼ Vincent at the age of thirteen. This photo was taken around the time he left his first boarding school.

▲ The influence of the French Protestant reformer John Calvin (1509–64) was seen in France, Scotland, and the Netherlands. Presbyterianism was based on his teachings that faith must be based on The Bible and that man lacked free will.

▼ Vincent admired the work of British writer Charles Dickens (1812–70), who portrayed the lives of poor working people in his books.

First Job

When he left school, Vincent spoke only of wanting to paint. Two of his uncles were art dealers. His Uncle Cent arranged for Vincent to work in The Hague in the Goupil & Cie Gallery. Vincent became distracted by his religious interests, and he was fired. In 1873, Vincent worked in a gallery in London. He had an unhappy love affair, and his relationship with the gallery deteriorated. He transferred to Paris, but the conflict of interests remained. In 1876, he returned to England.

▶ Miners *(1880)*. Vincent believed, *"To get on with miners you have to identify with them and not give yourself airs and graces, otherwise you won't establish a rapport with them and gain their confidence."*

Beginning to Draw

Vincent was dismissed from his post as preacher because the Church did not approve of his lifestyle. Vincent then decided to pursue his art and drew the miners and their families. Theo offered to pay for Vincent to study art in Paris. During this time, Vincent produced a mass of pen-and-ink and pencil drawings. Theo encouraged him to copy reproductions of the works of the French painter Jean-François Millet (1814–75), who portrayed the lives of poor working people. He regarded their lives as blessed because of their sad, hard labor. Vincent then moved to Brussels, where he befriended the Dutch painter Anthon van Rappard (1858–92).

▶ The Angelus *(1859) by Jean–François Millet. Millet was devoted to portraying the hard life of the peasant farmers working the soil.*

▼ *This drawing,* The Angelus *(1880), is based on Millet's oil painting. Vincent wrote to Theo, "I feel the need to study the drawing of the figure from masters like Millet."*

Religion

Like his father, Vincent had a strong religious calling. When he returned to England, he taught in a poor working-class area but devoted much of his time to studying *The Bible*. He then worked as an apprentice lay preacher and returned to Amsterdam to continue his religious studies. Intent on devoting his life to ministering to the sick and poor, he moved to the Borinage, a poor mining area in Belgium. He slept in barns and gave his food and possessions away.

The Hague

1881 In Etten, Vincent discusses his future and artistic development with Theo. He decides not to return to Brussels and draws landscapes. Vincent falls in love with his cousin Kee. Visits The Hague and meets with Anton Mauve. Goes to Amsterdam to propose to Kee. Returns to The Hague and starts to paint. He quarrels with his father. **1882** Vincent moves to The Hague. He is taught painting techniques by Anton Mauve. He becomes involved with Sien. Theo supports him financially, and his Uncle Cornelis commissions twelve pen-and-ink drawings of The Hague.

Vincent's return to his parents' home in 1881 proved a turning point. His religious convictions had dominated his life, but his need to draw and paint was beginning to emerge. Up until this point, he had focused on sketching and drawing in a variety of media, but now, with the help of his uncle, he started to paint. His early choice of subjects included nature and peasants at work, a theme he was to pursue throughout his life.

▼ *Vincent fell in love with his widowed cousin Kee, who was raising her son as a single mother.*

▼ *Oil paint was now packaged in soft tin tubes, making it easier for artists to work outdoors.*

Different Techniques

Vincent's uncle encouraged him to explore his talent and gave him a set of watercolors in 1881. "What a wonderful thing watercolor is for expressing space," he declared, "the figure is in the atmosphere and comes to life." Watercolor paint is applied thinly in transparent washes so that the white of the paper shines through, giving an airy feel to the picture. Vincent soon experimented with oil paints too, which are applied in thicker layers, often using the brush strokes to build up a rich texture.

Kee

In the summer of 1881, while visiting his parents, Vincent met with his cousin Cornelia Adriana Vos-Stricker, known as Kee. She rejected his advances, and he went back to Amsterdam. Later, in autumn, determined to win her over, he returned to propose to her. She refused to see him. Determined to prove his love to her parents, Vincent placed his hand over the flames of a lamp, hoping this would force her to see him. Kee's father simply blew the lamp out — and Vincent's hope with it. He left feeling dejected.

Anton Mauve and The Hague School

A notable painter of animals and landscapes, Anton Mauve (1838–88) was a leading member of the Hague School. This group of painters wanted to convey mood and depict nature as they saw it. The painters were also known as the Gray School because their color was subdued with a preference for gray. In 1881, Vincent studied with Anton, who taught him oil painting techniques.

▶ Shepherdess *(1880) by Anton Mauve. In an attempt to revive the naturalistic approach of the seventeenth-century Dutch painters, Mauve painted everyday life, landscapes, and seascapes.*

Sien

While living in the Hague, Vincent met Clasina Maria Hoornik, a poor pregnant woman known as Sien. Vincent's sympathy for those who had fallen on hard times reemerged. He wrote to Theo: "I took the woman for a model, and have worked with her all winter. I could not pay her the full wages of a model, but that did not prevent me paying her rent, and, thank God, I have been able thus far to protect her and her child from hunger." The studies he did of Sien and her children were laden with emotion compared with his earlier drawings of the miners. He captured the intimacy of domestic life while expressing hardship and despair. Their relationship suffered as Vincent's work developed, and the following year Vincent left Sien and headed north.

◄ *Detail of* Woman Sewing, with a Girl *(1883). While in The Hague, Vincent made over fifty drawings of Sien.*

▲ Beach at Scheveningen in Stormy Weather *(1882). Van Gogh's interest in underlying abstract form and energetic brush work are evident in this early work.*

▼ Self-Portrait *(c. 1884) by Anton Mauve. He was instrumental in van Gogh's development as a painter.*

Nuenen

1883 At the end of the year, Vincent returns to live with his parents in Nuenen for the next two years.

1884 Vincent nurses his mother, who is bedridden with a broken leg. Much to his parents' objection, he proposes to marry their neighbor's daughter, who attempts suicide by poisoning. The painter Anton van Rappard visits. He studies the relationship between color and music and is particularly interested in the music of Wagner.

During the years Vincent lived with his parents, he produced over two hundred paintings. Many were of his favorite subjects of peasants at work and landscapes. His parents allowed him to use a building attached to their house as a studio. Vincent continued to learn and develop, studying Delacroix's theories on art. His technique became more confident and fluent.

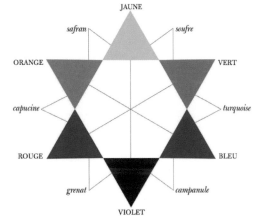

◀ *As factories increased and farming decreased, farm laborers moved from farm to farm to find work.*

Advances in Agriculture

Between the end of the eighteenth century and the beginning of the twentieth century, the partial mechanization of farming techniques was the main development to affect agriculture. Steam-powered plowing, horse-powered harvesting, new fertilizers, and research into plant diseases all evolved to make farming more efficient and productive. The availability of labor or the lack of it was one of the factors that spurred inventors to produce labor-saving machines.

▲ *The art critic Charles Blanc (1813–82) designed this color system showing primary and secondary colors. His* Grammar of Painting, and Engraving *(1879) was read by many artists, including van Gogh.*

Color Theory

The primary colors red, yellow, and blue cannot be acquired through mixing but produce all other colors when mixed. When two primary colors are mixed, the secondary colors, orange, green, and purple, are made. Complementary colors lie opposite each other on the color chart.

Peasant Studies

Like the one of his favorite writers, the French novelist Émile Zola (1840–1902), Vincent had a great feeling of compassion for the hard lives of poor workers. He tried to express the idea that through the honesty of their hard physical existence, peasants gained dignity. During this period, he had two particular favorite themes: the workers in the field and weavers at work.

▶ Farmers Planting Potatoes *(1884). Van Gogh was moved by the poverty he found, saying, "Here, it is the sick who tend the sick, the poor who befriend the poor."*

The Weaver

Weavers had been a popular theme with seventeenth-century Dutch artists. Van Gogh painted weavers hoping to draw attention to them as valid subject matter for contemporary artists. Theo's unenthusiastic response caused friction between them. Vincent accused Theo of not trying hard enough to sell his work. Going against Theo's advice to abandon the weavers, Vincent painted ten oils on this subject.

▼ Weaver Facing Right *(1884). This painting is a historical record of a dying cottage industry. The Industrial Revolution was rapidly replacing weavers with mechanized looms.*

▲ *Most of the people living in Brabant were employed in the textile industry.*

The Industrial Revolution

The process that changed the basis of the European economy from an agricultural to an industrial economy was called the Industrial Revolution. It started around 1750 but gained momentum between 1815 and 1914. Muscle, water, and wind power had been the driving forces, but the mechanized inventions in the textile industry, which enabled faster and therefore greater productivity, led the way to one of the most significant turning points in men's lives. Few cities existed in the eighteenth century because labor was needed on the land. Manual labor, whether tilling fields, mining, or making clothes, was the order of the day. People and animals worked hard. The invention of the steam engine was the key to the Industrial Revolution. Factories were built in towns, and as farming became more mechanized, the workers moved off the land into towns, and cities evolved. Mass production and cheaper goods followed.

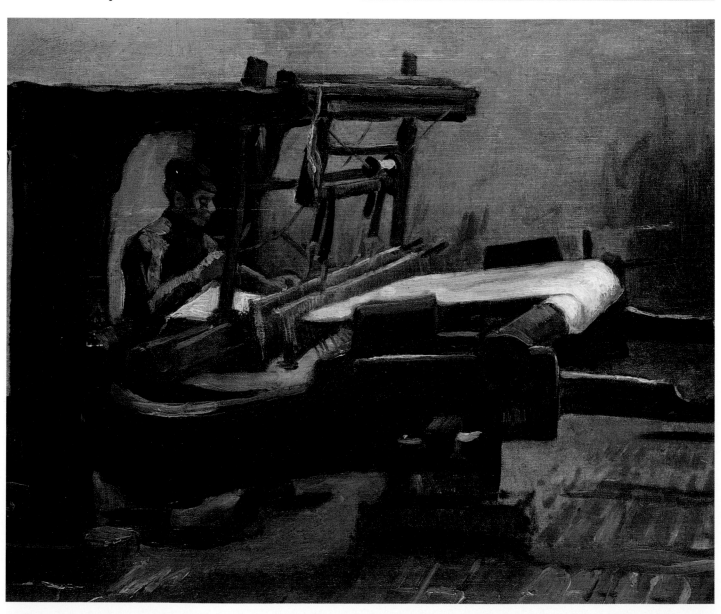

The Potato Eaters

1885 Van Gogh's father dies of a stroke on March 26. Van Gogh quarrels with his sister and moves into the studio in the house of the sacristan. He paints *The Potato Eaters*, his first significant masterpiece. Rappard is critical of his lithographs. Their friendship deteriorates. Van Gogh visits the Rijksmuseum and is impressed with the works of Rembrandt and Hals. He moves to Antwerp for six months. **1886** Van Gogh enrolls in the Academy of Fine Art in Antwerp. He objects to their academic teaching. He becomes ill from malnutrition and heavy smoking. He moves to Paris and is taken in by Theo. The Academy demotes him to the beginners' class.

Although Vincent painted some landscapes and still lifes of rustic pots, his interest in the lives of the workers continued to be his favorite theme. During the early part of 1885, he did many portrait studies of peasant men and women digging, sweeping, and washing clothes. These portraits were painted with strong, loose brush work reminiscent of the old masters Frans Hals (c. 1581–1666) and Rembrandt Harmenszoon van Rijn (1606–69).

▲ *The lighting from the oil lamp creates a subdued atmosphere emphasizing the hard life poor peasants led.*

▼ The Potato Eaters *(1885). Van Gogh did numerous compositional sketches before embarking on the final piece.*

The Potato Eaters

This dark painting encompasses Vincent's passionate feelings about the lives of the workers. "Indeed I have tried very hard to convey to the observer the idea that these people, who are eating potatoes by lamplight, reaching into the bowl with their hands, use the same hands to till the soil. The painting therefore conveys the idea of their manual work and as a consequence of this that their meal has been honestly earned." He wanted to depict reality as he saw it.

Socialist Ideals

▶ *In 1850, Karl Marx, a German philosopher, published* The Class Struggles in France, 1848–1850. Das Kapital *was published in 1867.*

The revolution in the mechanical world brought about social changes that disadvantaged the workers. Karl Marx (1818–83), a German philosopher and economist, together with Friedrich Engels (1820–95), spoke out against the development of capitalism, expressing their ideas in *The Communist Manifesto* in 1848. Capitalists, such as factory owners, were becoming wealthy at the expense of the proletariat, or working class, driving a gulf of resentment between employers and employees. Marx and Engels had a vision for a classless society in which property was no longer privately owned but owned communally. A revolution in which the working class overturned the power base of the capitalists was the only way they could see to achieve equality and democracy.

From Antwerp to Paris

Vincent arrived in Antwerp carrying *The Potato Eaters* in his suitcase. He attempted to sell his pictures and visited museums where he discovered the work of Hals and Peter Paul Rubens (1577–1640). He found some Japanese prints and started to collect them. These discoveries were to inspire him in his use of color, brush work, and composition. He enrolled in the Academy of Fine Art but quit four weeks later. Although he had money to buy Japanese prints, he was suffering from malnutrition. He finally left for Paris to meet Theo.

▼ *Portrait of Émile Zola (1867–8) by Eduoard Manet (1832–83). The detailed realism in Zola's novels exposed many of the social problems of the time.*

▼ The Meagre Company *(1633–7) by Frans Hals. Van Gogh was inspired by the quick and choppy brushwork Hals used in his paintings.*

▲ *In this painting, titled* Still Life with Bible *(1885), we can see Zola's novel* La Joie de Vivre *placed near* The Bible. *It shows van Gogh's interest in the philosophy of the Naturalist movement led by Zola.*

Rubens and Hals

Rubens was a Flemish Baroque artist who was the leading painter of his day. He lived and studied in Italy, where he copied the work of Italian masters. Hals, another Flemish painter, concentrated on portraiture. Like Rubens, Hals preferred to work with loose brushwork. In his later work, detail was less important than the spontaneous, expressive gesture, and in many parts, his figures appeared sketchy. Their style inspired Vincent.

1886 Vincent moves to Paris in March and studies in the studio of Cormon with Henri de Toulouse-Lautrec and Émile Bernard. Trying the pointillist technique, he paints views of Paris and still life groups. The last exhibition of the Société des Artistes Indépendants shows works of the Pointillists.

1887 He paints outdoors and produces more than ten self-portraits.

Paris

In Paris, Vincent lived with Theo in an apartment in Montmartre. At the time Vincent arrived in Paris, the Impressionists had mounted their last exhibition and new Postimpressionist movements, such as pointillism, or divisionism, were emerging. Vincent met with many of the important Impressionists and other artists like Georges Seurat and Paul Gauguin. Gauguin was to become a close friend, and they exhibited together, along with Henri de Toulouse-Lautrec.

Experiments in Style

In Paris, Vincent soon experimented with new ideas and techniques but not without arguing about their validity. His palette, inspired by the Impressionist use of light and color, soon became more vibrant and clear. He still kept his own individual style and also took the chance to study and copy the works found in the Louvre museum of the French painter Eugène Delacroix (1798–1863), who was generally considered one of the forerunners of impressionism and divisionism.

▲ Self-Portrait with Dark Felt Hat *(1886). Vincent described himself as a man so wrinkled and furrowed that he appeared to be ten years older than his thirty-three years.*

▶ Impression: Sunrise *(c. 1873) by Claude Monet seemed like an unfinished work. For this reason, a journalist, intending to criticize the work, called it an "impressionist" painting. The movement became known as "impressionism."*

▶ Interior of a Restaurant *(1887). This painting shows Vincent experimenting with the pointillist technique and using a brighter palette than his earlier paintings of miners.*

▲ *Montmartre became the center of artistic and bohemian life in Paris. This poster is an advertisement for the Moulin Rouge dance hall. It became one of the most popular night clubs in the area by the turn of the century.*

Impressionism

From the late 1860's, artists such as Claude Monet (1840–1926) and Camille Pissarro (1830–1903) took their canvases into the field so they could capture the moment. They no longer wanted their work to carry moral or social messages. Instead, they focused on recreating optical effects. Their interests paralleled the discovery that white light was a combination of rainbow colors. Two colors could be seen separately on a static wheel, but when spun, they fused together to create the impression of one. The Impressionists, as they came to be known, used this notion in their response to light. Instead of modeling gradated tones to show light on a solid surface, they broke up the colors so they mixed together on the retina.

Pointillism

Pointillism is the technique of painting countless tiny daubs of color. The sizes of the dots, painted in a primary color, are changed according to the size of the painting, and the tones are carefully adjusted to blend or contrast. When viewed from a distance, the colors appear to merge, creating the impression of new colors that heighten the quality of light. This technique was practiced by both Georges Seurat (1859–91) and Paul Signac (1863–1935), although they preferred to call it divisionism.

▼ Sunday Afternoon on the Island of La Grande Jatte *(1884–6) by Georges Seurat. Using the technique of juxtaposing tiny dots of complementary colors, known as pointillism, Seurat painted a scene of Parisians relaxing by the Seine River.*

▲ Agostina Segatori Sitting in the Café du Tambourin *(1887). Van Gogh painted this portrait of the proprietor of the Café du Tambourin. He exhibited his own works and organized an exhibition of Japanese prints at this Parisian café.*

1887 Vincent has a brief love affair with Agostina Segatori, the owner of the Café du Tambourin and a former model of Corot and Degas. He paints a portrait of Segatori inspired by Toulouse-Lautrec's portraits of café life. He mounts an exhibition with Émile Bernard, Gauguin, and Toulouse-Lautrec at the Grand Bouillon Restaurant du Chalet on the Boulevard de Clichy. They were known as the "Peintres du Petit Boulevard." He produces over a dozen self-portraits using his new pointillist technique. Paints *Portrait of Père Tanguy*.

Japanese Prints

In 1886, Vincent had painted scenes of Paris. The next year, his interest in bright color and complementary contrasts, suggested by impressionism, was strengthened in his work. This technique of placing daubs of complementary colors, such as blues against oranges, reds against greens, or purples against yellows, can be seen in many of his paintings from this time period. In the 1850s, a fascination with Japan, which had been closed off from Western culture since 1635, flourished in the West, and ports were opened for trade. Vincent collected Japanese prints, and his interest in them emerges in his work.

◄ *This nineteenth-century print portrays the arrival of the U.S. fleet in Tokyo Bay and the locals in their small boats going out to meet them. The arrival of the fleet ended the Japanese policy of isolation and allowed Westerners to come into contact with Japanese culture.*

▼ *This print by Keisai Eisen (1790–1848) was seen by van Gogh on the cover of the special Japan issue of the periodical* Paris Illustré *in 1886.*

Fascination with Japan
In 1867, Paris hosted the World Exhibition. Interest in the Japanese stand gave rise to Parisian women dressing in kimonos, using fans, and buying Japanese screens. The interest in Japanese art could be seen in the compositions of the Impressionists. Later, the painter Monet even built a Japanese-style bridge in his garden.

Van Gogh's Japonaiseries
At this time Japonaiserie, the art of copying Japanese woodcuts, was established in France. Vincent wrote, "I envy the Japanese artist for the incredible neat clarity which all their works have." Vincent was particularly interested in the work of Ando Hiroshige (1797–1858), one of the last real print masters. Vincent interpreted rather than copied many of the prints he collected. He did not mimic the smooth application of color or copy them accurately but preferred to translate the images into a personal form.

▲ The Courtesan (after Keisai Eisen) *(1887). Van Gogh traced Eisen's print, enlarged it, and freely interpreted the patterns and colors on the kimono. He added his own border based on other prints around the central panel.*

Père Tanguy

Père Tanguy was a minor art dealer and paint seller. To help Vincent and other Impressionists, he took paintings in exchange for new canvases and paint. Vincent painted three portraits of him, all with very similar compositions, in which he surrounds the simple frontal pose of Tanguy with a decorative backdrop of Japanese prints. The flattening of the picture plane shows his admiration for the graphic decorative style of Hiroshige. The palettes used in all three works are notably brighter. At this time, ready-mixed paints were being manufactured and were no doubt sold by Tanguy.

◀ Van Gogh's portrait of Père Tanguy *(1887). Van Gogh chose an unpretentious pose to express the simple working-class origins of the sitter.*

▶ *Toulouse-Lautrec (1864–1901) was also inspired by Japanese prints. He designed this poster,* Divan Japonais *(1893), for a café in Paris. The name of the café was inspired by the Japanese craze.*

Return to the South

The two years van Gogh spent in Paris saw his work going through an amazing transformation. He had perfected the use of complementary contrast he had learned from the Impressionists. He had integrated the freer fragmented brushwork of the Pointillists with the flat decorative elements from Japanese prints. It had been a positive time, yet Vincent became depressed in the dark winter months and was not at home in big cities despite the stimulation of the artists he met and the museums he visited. At the beginning of 1888, he decided it was time to return to the country. He yearned for the sun and vibrant light, now an important element in his work, and he set off for the South.

▲ Walk Along the Banks of the Seine Near Asnières *(1887). Vincent spent a lot of time outdoors in the sunshine, whether working or simply taking long walks. When winter came, he decided to move to the warmer climate of the South.*

Arles

1888 In February, Vincent leaves Paris to live in the South. He arrives in Arles and focuses on drawing and painting landscapes. He travels to the coast and produces seascapes with boats. He also takes up portrait painting again.

▼ *Alphonse Daudet (1840–97) retreated from the hectic city life of Paris and wrote stories about Provençal life. Born in Nîmes, he is the author of two still very famous books,* Lettres de mon Moulin *and* Tartarin de Tarascon, *both set in Provence.*

After painting two hundred pictures in two years, Vincent left the busy city life, where he was never really at home. Inspired by the novels of Alphonse Daudet, he headed to Provence, where the warm colors of the southern landscape appealed to his eye. He settled in Arles and went back to painting landscapes outdoors, but this time he merged the techniques and heightened palette he had developed in Paris. In time, he made friends and started painting portraits again. As a result, he produced a most brilliant collection of paintings, including seascapes.

▲ *Hiroshige was famous for the poetic atmosphere in his Japanese landscape prints. Van Gogh was greatly interested in his work.*

▼ *Detail of* Fishing Boats on the Beach at Saintes-Maries *(1888). Van Gogh had long wanted to visit the coast and produced several seascapes.*

Blossoming Orchards

In a letter to his sister, he wrote: "I have no need for Japanese art here, since I tell myself I am in Japan, and only need to open my eyes and take everything in before me." Vincent painted the most Japanese motifs he could find, such as the spring blossoms of the peach trees, a favorite theme of the Japanese artist Hiroshige, but he now painted from life.

Life in Arles

When Vincent first arrived in Arles, he had little money, and he knew no one, so he had no immediate source of models. Instead, drawn by the wonderful vibrant colors in the landscape, he painted his new surroundings. He painted many different scenes, including the fields, orchards, and peasants at work. He also painted seascapes, in which he depicted the nearby drawbridge and boats in the harbor of Sainte-Maries-de-la-Mer.

▲ The Langlois Bridge at Arles with Women Washing *(1888). Van Gogh was fascinated by the graphic quality of the bridge, which was reminiscent of Japanese prints.*

Harvest Landscapes

Vincent spent much of his early time in Arles walking and painting in the fields. He painted at least ten pictures recording the harvest bathed in the exotic Mediterranean light. He had developed a process of first drawing and then exploring the subject further with color studies before doing the final picture. The preparation allowed him to work with speed and confidence, giving freshness to the final paintings. He was particularly pleased with the example shown below and wrote to Theo that the "canvas absolutely diminished all the rest."

Cézanne

The French Postimpressionist painter Paul Cézanne (1839–1906), now considered one of the most important artists of his time, developed a style that tended to reveal the geometric structure of landscapes and figures. His work was to herald many of the modern art movements that followed. Vincent first met Cézanne at Tanguy's shop. Although their styles were quite different, their works were later exhibited alongside each other.

▼ Harvest at La Crau, with Montmajour in the Background *(1888). The Provençal land, with flat areas and hills, enabled van Gogh to paint panoramic views.*

▲ Mont Sainte-Victoire *(1885–87) by Paul Cézanne. By using fragmented blocks of colors, carefully balanced in tone and hue, Cézanne created a new way of depicting space.*

Studio of the South

1888 In September, Vincent makes a series of night paintings. He moves into the Yellow House. Theo comes into money and supports him and provides the necessary funds to furnish the Yellow House.
In October, Paul Gauguin moves to Arles, and they work and live together in the Yellow House. Vincent has a mental breakdown after a row with Gauguin. He cuts off his ear. He is discovered by the police and hospitalized. Gauguin leaves and lets Theo know of Vincent's condition.

Vincent and Gauguin had both left Paris after a bleak winter. Vincent made his way south, and Gauguin went west to Brittany in search of a simple, more primitive life style. During this period, an important correspondence developed between them in which they exchanged ideas about the symbolic and emotional use of colors. They were both interested in the compositional devices of bold outlines on flat planes employed by the Japanese.

▼ Vincent's Bedroom in Arles *(1888). This painting, executed in Arles, was the first of three oil paintings on this subject. The other two versions were painted from memory.*

▶ *Vincent's House in Arles, known as* The Yellow House *(1888). Vincent hoped to establish an artist's commune here with Gauguin.*

The Yellow House
In May, Vincent rented four rooms in the wing of a large house. "My house", he writes, "is painted butter yellow on the outside and has solid green shutters . . . inside all the walls are painted white and the floor is tiled in red. Yet the most striking thing is the glaring blue sky. Inside the house I can really live and breathe and think and paint." He dreamed of establishing a commune in the Yellow House where artists could focus on their work and not be worried by the material world. He had hoped to establish it with Gauguin's help.

▼ *The book* Madam Chrysanthéme, *by the French author Pierre Loti (1850–1923), contained descriptions of Japanese interiors that clearly suggested the way van Gogh decorated the house.*

Van Gogh's Room at Arles
In October, Vincent began to depict his room. In a letter to Theo about the painting, he wrote ". . . it's just simply my bedroom, only here color is to do everything, and giving by its simplification a grander style to things, is to be suggestive here of rest or of sleep in general. In a word, looking at the picture ought to rest the brain, or rather the imagination". He did two sketches and three oil paintings of his room. Described in at least thirteen letters, this piece was one of Vincent's favorites.

Sunflowers

Vincent planned to decorate the house with a series of paintings with linked themes. "Gauguin, if he comes, will have white walls with a decoration of great yellow sunflowers," he wrote to Theo when planning the artists' commune. As soon as he heard that Gauguin was arriving, his melancholy lifted, and he produced four sunflower paintings. He had intended to hang them in Gauguin's room but rejected two, which he didn't even sign. Vincent described his technique as "light on light," a method of building up layers of subtly varied shades of rich golds. Sadly, their relationship did not reflect the overwhelming joy expressed in these paintings, which were produced in anticipation of their meeting.

▲ An illustration depicting the famous characters from Les Misérables, *the novel written by the great Romantic French author Victor Hugo (1802–85). Gauguin wrote that he, as well as other artists of the time, had much in common with Hugo's heroic character, Jean Valjean.*

▲ Still Life: Vase with Twelve Sunflowers *(1888). Van Gogh painted only seven of the twelve sunflower still lifes he had planned.*

▶ Self-Portrait, Les Misérables *(1888) by Paul Gauguin. In this self-portrait, dedicated to Vincent, Gaugin portrays himself in the role of the outlaw from Victor Hugo's* Les Misérables. *It is, of course, an ironic reference, and the title has to be understood as "those who are in poverty and misery."*

Gauguin

Paul Gauguin (1848–1903) started his adult life as a stockbroker. He had seen the first exhibition of Impressionist paintings and collected them. He started to paint and was soon exhibiting. He met Vincent at Theo's in Paris and was to become a friend and mentor. When Vincent learned that Gauguin had became ill and depressed, he invited Gauguin to join him in Arles. Within weeks, however, heated arguments had broken out. Vincent reputedly attacked Gauguin with a razor. The next day, when Gauguin heard that Vincent had cut off his ear, he left Arles, and they never met again.

Passion for Portraits

Throughout his life, Vincent was passionate about painting portraits. The traditional style of Dutch seventeenth-century portraits as seen in the work of Rembrandt and Hals was still popular. He wanted to paint his sitters as they really were and to express his feelings about them. In his early works of peasants, the skin was modeled in muted tones. Later, his treatment of skin underwent a radical change as he introduced the complementary contrasts learned from the Impressionists and applied paint with textured, rhythmic brushwork.

Passion for Portraits

Vincent painted the poor peasants to show his concern for them as a social group, but many of his portraits are of individuals he had struck up a special bond with, such as Père Tanguy, Dr. Gachet, and Madame Ginoux. "What impassions me most — much more than all the rest of my métier — is the portrait, the modern portrait. I seek it in color, and surely I am not the only one to seek it in this direction. I should like — mind you, far be it from me to say that I shall be able to do it, although this is what I am aiming at — I should like to paint portraits which would appear after a century to people living then as apparitions."

◄ La Mousmé, Sitting (1888). Vincent was attracted to paint the unknown Provençal girl because he thought she had the appearance of a "Japanese girl."

Color and Music

Vincent's interest in color went beyond the popular color theories of the day. He saw in color a parallel with the emotional power of music and aspired to "make painting into something like the music of Berlioz or Wagner." Richard Wagner (1813–83) was a German composer whose works expressed turbulent emotions similar to Vincent's tempestuous works. Wagner had developed theories relating the musical quality in poetry with music.

▲ Van Gogh greatly admired the satirical cartoons of the artist Honoré Daumier (1808–79). He particularly admired Daumier's figure drawing for its direct expression and characterization.

▼ Vincent admired the emotional and psychological power of Wagner's music and tried to fill his color with the same strength of feeling.

▶ Portrait of the Postman Joseph Roulin *(1888). Vincent's portraits of the postman reflect his respect for his friend.*

▼ Portrait of Milliet, Second Lieutenant of the Zouaves *(1888). Vincent and Milliet spent much time together. Vincent depicted him in his uniform and also gave him drawing lessons.*

The Zouave

The French army had small group of light infantry men, many from Algeria, known as the Zouaves. The French had occupied Algiers in 1830 and later declared Northern Algeria as part of France. Although they were part of a European army, their uniform was distinctly Arabian in its style. They wore large red baggy pantaloons with yellow shirts and neatly cut blue jackets. The portraits of a Zouave that Vincent produced were strong in composition and dramatic. Many years later, Paul-Eugène Milliet, the second lieutenant of the Zouaves who was portrayed by van Gogh, was interviewed by a writer who recognized him from his portrait. He recalled that Vincent did not sketch out the portrait but did it very quickly and still captured an accurate likeness. Milliet said that he had enjoyed Vincent's company.

The Roulin Family

During his time in Arles, Vincent became friends with the postman, Joseph Roulin. Vincent may have met him when he sent a parcel of paintings to his brother Theo in Paris. Joseph Roulin and his wife, Augustine, were very kind to Vincent and invited him to their home many times. In a letter to Theo, Vincent wrote that he was working on a portrait of Joseph Roulin. He likened him to the great ancient Greek philosopher Socrates and wrote that he was "a man more interesting than most." Gradually, Vincent painted the whole Roulin family, including the baby.

▼ La Berceuse *(1889). Madame Roulin, the wife of the postman, was regarded as the archetypal woman and mother. In this painting, she is depicted holding the cord to rock the cradle.*

Cafés

Since the seventeenth century, cafés had been important meeting places for the exchange of ideas on politics, philosophy, and culture. In the nineteenth century, cafés were also the hub of the creative and intellectual life of the period. Parisian cafés, in particular, became famous as meeting places for the writers, poets, artists, and philosophers of the day. Vincent and Gauguin often visited the cafés in Arles. Places like Café Terrace on the Place Du Forum were also meeting places for illicit activity. Vincent saw "the café as a place where you can ruin yourself, go mad, and commit a crime."

▲ *The Procope opened in 1686; it is the oldest café in Paris. Voltaire and Napoléon were among its clients.*

Night Life

Gauguin and Vincent spent many evenings at their favorite café, the Café de la Gare, which was run by the Ginoux family. There they embarked on many heated debates on the aesthetics of contemporary painting. Vincent slept during the day so he could paint the cafés at night. *The Night Café in the Place Lamartine in Arles*, with its strong yellow lighting, is another example of Vincent's use of color as a means to convey his emotional response to his subject matter. He had "tried to describe the terrible passions of humanity by means of green and red."

▼ *Gauguin, as well as Vincent, painted the portrait of Madame Ginoux at the Café de la Gare. This is a detail of Gauguin's painting titled* The Café at Arles *(1888).*

◀ *Vincent called this painting,* The Night Café in the Place Lamartine in Arles, *"one of the ugliest I have done."*

The Café Terrace

Vincent's nocturnal painting was not confined to painting well-lit interiors. The Baroque painters had enjoyed painting interiors by artificial light, and the Impressionists had taken their easels outdoors in daylight. Night scenes would have been based on sketches but painted in daylight. Vincent, however, was the first to paint outdoors at night. In order to create enough light to paint by, Vincent set up candles on his easel and sometimes on the brim of his hat. Vincent wrote to his sister Wil, "Here you have a night picture without any black in it, done with nothing but beautiful blue and violet and green, and in these surroundings the lighted square acquires a pale sulphur and greenish citron-yellow color." This painting (right) is the first of three nocturnal star-spangled sky paintings he was to do and one of the strongest images he created.

▲ Café Terrace on the Place du Forum, Arles, at Night (1888). *"The night,"* claimed van Gogh, *"is livelier and richer in color than day."*

▼ Street Scene, at Five in the Afternoon *(1887) by Louis Annqetin, one of Vincent's friends, who had lived on the Boulevard and Avenue de Clichy.*

▼ *A caricature of Maupassant. During the period from 1880–90, a time of intense productivity, he published over three hundred works.*

▲ *Detail of* A Still Life with Plaster Statuette *(1887). Van Gogh liked to show his literary preferences in his paintings.*

Maupassant

Vincent had read of a similar scene of "a starlit night in Paris with the brightly lighted cafés of the Boulevard" in Guy de Maupassant's *Bel-Ami* (1885). Maupassant (1850–93) was a member of Zola's group of Naturalist writers. For them, human behavior could be explained by natural or material causes and by social environment. Maupassant wrote over three hundred short stories, three travel books, and six novels. His stories were usually based around everyday episodes but revealed the hidden side of human nature. His waspish sense of humor added spice to his objective approach to writing.

Mental Turmoil

1888 In December, van Gogh and Gauguin argue violently after going to Montpellier to see *Bonjour Monsieur Courbet* by Gustav Courbet, the French realist painter. The police take Vincent to a hospital, where he stays for two weeks. Gauguin leaves immediately, and they rarely communicate after this event.

▼ Self-Portrait with Bandaged Ear *(1889). Van Gogh painted this powerful self-portrait when he left the hospital after mutilating his ear after his argument with Gauguin.*

Back in October, Vincent had so looked forward to Gauguin's arrival, but by December, their relationship was in a terminal state. It is not certain whether this stemmed from their artistic disputes or whether their self-centered personalities were the basis for the "exaggerated tensions" that quickly developed between them. When he left, Gauguin claimed it was the incompatibility of their personalities, but he had accused Vincent of being a romantic and criticized him, declaring, "In applying color he loves the impulsive, while I hate disorderly undertakings."

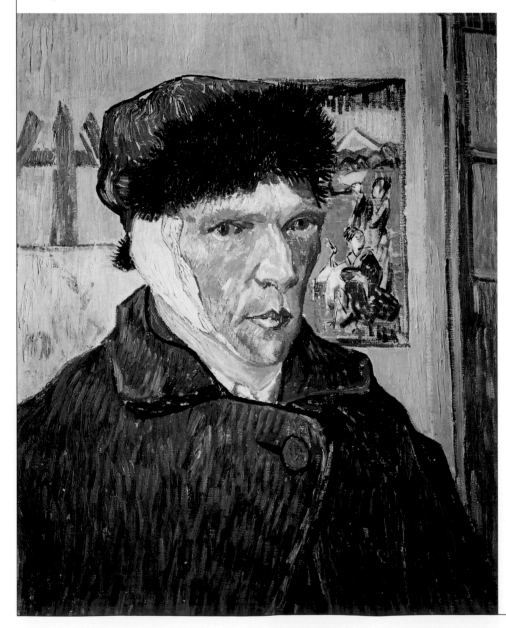

▼ Portrait of Dr. Félix Rey *(1889). He took care of van Gogh after the ear incident.*

Cause or Effect?

It is debatable whether the increasingly unstable state of Vincent's mind caused the breakdown of his friendship with Gaugin. The end of their relationship may have contributed to Vincent's mental troubles. When Vincent cut off part of his left ear, he wrapped it in a handkerchief and gave it to a woman on the street. Then he went home to bed. The next day, he was taken to a hospital by police. Vincent apparently suffered from epilepsy, alcoholism, and schizophrenia. At this time, society regarded the mentally ill as simply mad and dangerous.

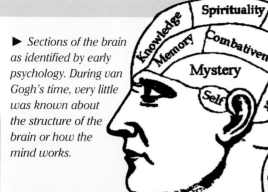

▶ *Sections of the brain as identified by early psychology. During van Gogh's time, very little was known about the structure of the brain or how the mind works.*

Psychiatry

Psychiatry is the study of mental disorders, which include psychosis, neurosis, psychosomatic disorders, and addictions. When Vincent was being diagnosed, the study of mental disorders was in its infancy. His condition was described as "an acute mania with general delirium (and) irregularly recurring epileptic attacks." There was very little understanding, let alone diagnosis and treatment, of mental illness. People suffering from mental disorders were held in lunatic asylums and often kept in mechanical restraining devices. In about 1860, views of the scientist Charles Darwin (1809–82) that insanity was an incurable, degenerative hereditary disease held back the real development of psychiatry. Those who were considered physically and morally dangerous were sent to lunatic asylums for custody or control; others were left with their families or kept in workhouses as a cheaper solution.

Two Chairs

Art historians have debated about these paintings of the two artists' chairs and the possible symbolic interpretation of them as portraits of Gauguin and van Gogh himself. They are frequently displayed together in a back-to-back position to symbolize a conflict between their two personalities. In his letters, van Gogh comments on the emphasis on the complementary colors in the "somber reddish-brown wood," against "the seat of greenish straw" which was the key to the expression of his feelings for his subject.

▲ Paul Gauguin's Armchair *(1888). This chair, lit by two lights and holding two books, expresses van Gogh's admiration for Gauguin's intellect. In this work, van Gogh uses his friend's style.*

Artist's Fit

Vincent was described as disheveled, eccentric, and frequently depressed. He suffered from mood swings often invoked by periods of excessive drinking. Gauguin wrote, "In spite of a few differences I can't be angry with a good chap who is ill and suffering and calling for me." Vincent himself expressed some concern about his own behavior. He wrote to Theo, "I hope I have just had simply an artist's fit".

▲ *Van Gogh smoked his pipe in bed on the last day before he died.*

▲ Vincent's Chair with his Pipe *(1888). The steeply tilted floor, the abandoned pipe, and the awkward perspective create a disturbing dynamic.*

Saint-Rémy

Vincent's dreams of his friendship with Gauguin and establishing an artists' commune were shattered. Suffering from persecution mania, he told Theo "I don't dare to ask other painters to come here after what has happened. They risk losing their mind, just like me." During this period in Provence, Vincent produced a vast collection of brilliant paintings. They varied in subject matter from landscapes, portraits, night scenes, interiors, and still lifes to more copies of the paintings of Millet.

1889 Van Gogh leaves the hospital but returns after recurring hallucinations. Paints in the Yellow House. Due to a petition raised by the citizens of Arles, van Gogh is hospitalized. He enters an asylum in Saint-Rémy, near Arles. Theo pays for two rooms so Vincent can paint at the asylum. Starts Cypress series. An attack impairs his memory. His work starts to receive recognition. He exhibits ten paintings in the Salon des Indépendants. He is asked to exhibit in Brussels and wants to return north. During another attack, he attempts to eat paint.

▲ *Van Gogh spent fifty-three weeks in the Saint-Rémy Asylum.*

▼ The Vision after the Sermon, Jacob Wrestling with the Angel *(1888) by Gauguin is an example of a symbolist painting. Many consider it one of his most important works.*

The Asylum

"I finally feel incapable of taking a new studio . . . neither here in Arles, nor anywhere else. I would like to stay temporarily in the asylum." Theo was about to marry, and Vincent was worried he would lose the support of his caring brother. Feeling unable to cope, Vincent entered the mental asylum Saint-Paul-de-Mausole Sanatorium in St-Rémy. After a stable period, Vincent suffered another fit, during which he attempted to eat paint. Under the care of Dr. Peyron, he was diagnosed with epilepsy, and as the fits became more frequent, they were often violent and accompanied by hallucinations.

▲ The Vestibule of the Asylum *(1889). Van Gogh was allowed to paint in the asylum. He created this work with chalk and ink.*

Symbolism

During the nineteenth century, Symbolism came about as a reaction against Impressionism and Realism. It aimed to bring the material and spiritual realms together in art, expressing abstract ideas through painting. The movement was connected to the same movement in poetry that aimed to use language as an expression of the inner life. Symbolist painters, whose styles varied, used color and design to communicate ideas.

▲ Irises *(1889), with its contrast of warm and cool colors, is one of the paintings Vincent created in the garden of the asylum.*

▼ *The Eiffel Tower was the central attraction of the 1889 Universal Exposition in Paris.*

Irises

While in the sanatorium, Vincent was encouraged to get fresh air. In the garden, he discovered the vibrant color of the flowers there. Examining nature in close-up presented him with an ideal opportunity to play with complementary contrast: the silver grey-green with the bitter orange earth and the violet with the warm yellow splashes.

Exhibitions

Vincent exhibited in several venues during this period. In March, he was to receive the acclaim of his fellow artists when he showed ten paintings at the Salon des Indèpendants. The group was started in reaction to the official Salon because it would not welcome new styles in art.

▶ *Van Gogh wanted to keep the treatment of this portrait of Madame Ginoux,* L'Arlesienne *(1888), bold and simple. Once more, he used the complementary contrasts between red and green and violet-blue and yellow.*

Landscapes

The new development of packaging paint in small metal tubes allowed for easy transportation and enabled painters to work in the open air. They could now respond to the ever-changing light and movement in the skies. Vincent much preferred to work outside rather than trying to work from his memory. It gave him a vehicle for expressing his innermost feelings, and in this he became recognized as a forerunner to Expressionism.

▼ *Detail of* Starry Night. *Impasto is the application of thick paint with either a brush or a palette knife to create texture.*

Impasto

Vincent was greatly interested by the work of the French painter Adolphe Monticelli (1824–86) and also studied the works of Rembrandt, who used a mixture of impasto and fine glazes. Monticelli used thick impasto to create heavily textured swirls of paint, a motif often employed by Vincent. This technique could only be achieved with oil paint because watercolor and tempera were both too thin. They could make swirl marks on the paper but could not create the physical thickness of paint that oil and the recently developed acrylic paints permitted.

▶ Agony in the Garden *(1889) by Gauguin. Van Gogh believed in painting from life and argued violently with Gauguin about his practice of painting quasi-religious scenes from imagination.*

▲ Olive Grove *(1889). At the time, van Gogh was suffering "from a terrible loneliness," and his brushwork reflected his mood. It became more restless than the painting he executed during the happier time he had in Arles.*

▼ *As an image from the film* Lust for Life *shows, Vincent was happiest when he was painting outdoors, even at night or in bad weather. Kirk Douglas played van Gogh.*

Olive Groves

The olive series was done partly in response to Gauguin's preference for painting from imagination. Vincent believed in working from life, and this difference in their approaches certainly contributed to their arguments. Vincent saw the olive tree as the southern equivalent of the willow of the north. In the painting *Olive Grove*, Vincent used comma-like brushstrokes throughout the painting, giving all objects in the work the same treatment. The waving brushwork adds life and rhythm to the trees, and at the same time, it suggests the gusts of mistral, the strong wind that blows in Provence.

Landscapes

Starry Night

Painted while he was living in the asylum at Saint-Rémy, at a time when his behavior was very erratic, *Starry Night* is one of Vincent's most famous works. It is not certain whether he painted *Starry Night*, with its stunning night effect, from life or based it on studies he had done earlier. Vincent exaggerated certain rhythms and shapes, often mirrored in the brush strokes, thus creating an extremely turbulent effect. Because Vincent said very little to Theo about this work, we can only guess at what inspired him. In this painting, a tall cypress tree lies in the foreground and a village, possibly Saint-Rémy, and the Alpilles mountains can be seen below the bright stars in the night sky.

▶ Starry Night *(1889). This work has been the subject of poems, novels, and Don McLean's famous song "Starry, Starry Night."*

▼ *Like obelisks, van Gogh's cypresses lead the eye to the heavens.*

Self-Portraits

Vincent painted as many as thirty-eight self-portraits during his short career. He painted twenty-nine during his stay in Paris, five in Arles, and four at the asylum in Saint-Rémy. The reason he painted so many self-portraits is simply that he could not afford to pay for models to pose for him. Vincent wrote that he wanted to paint men and women with a "vibration of colors" and that portraits should express "the thought, the soul of the model." His self-portraits, with penetrating eyes and intense energy, seem to have these qualities.

▲ *From as early as the sixth century B.C., artists have been identified by the tools of their trade.*

Self-Portraiture

When making a portrait study, the artist can find himself torn between the need to make a recognizable representation of the sitter, the desire to express the sitter's character, and the temptation to create an idealized statement about either the looks or the character of the sitter. This is particularly true when it comes to making a self-portrait. The artist sees himself as a mirror image; thus, the self-portrait is a distortion of the real image. Dürer and Rembrandt were among the first to portray a psychological awareness of themselves.

▶ Self-Portrait *(1660) by Rembrandt. The soft, glowing light is typical of the mystical lighting of Rembrandt's religious paintings.*

Van Gogh and Rembrandt

Rembrandt, a fellow Dutchman, was one of the artists whose work Vincent copied and admired greatly. Rembrandt was the leading portrait artist in Holland but was also recognized as an engraver, landscape painter, and painter of religious themes. Rembrandt is most admired for his rendering of *chiaroscuro* (see page 37) as well as for his rich textural brush work. His rendering of light and darkness went beyond capturing lighting effects he had observed and was endowed with a mystical glow as seen not only in his religious works but also in his self-portraits. It was Rembrandt's use of tone to create the rich glow of light that Vincent admired in his work. However, Vincent did not attempt to copy Rembrandt's work accurately but used the luminosity of hue with the vibratory effect of juxtaposing complementary colors to create a similar quality.

▲ *The Italian mathematician, philosopher, and astronomer Galileo (1564–1642) observed that we only see the length and width of an object but not its thickness. This can only be observed from the play of light and darkness on its surfaces. The technique of chiaroscuro in painting aimed to show this play of light and darkness.*

Self-Study

As in his later portraits, the focus in Vincent's self-portraits is on the eyes. They are so intensely focused that they look out with a piercing gaze at the viewer. We must not forget, however, that in making these paintings, he was gazing deeply into his own eyes. Compared with Rembrandt's, which convey a warm, sensuous man, Vincent's later self-portraits show a man who is clearly in inner turmoil.

▲ *Kirk Douglas in a scene from the 1956 film* Lust for Life, *a biography of Vincent van Gogh based on a novel.*

Change in Style

The early painting of *Self-Portrait with Grey Felt Hat* shows Rembrandt's influence in the tonal rendering of light and modeling of the face and hat. From van Gogh's letters, it appears that he was concerned with mapping his physical features as he saw them: "My forehead is marked with wrinkles, the lines on my face are those of a 40-year-old. . . ." Vincent was clearly not pursuing romantic ideals. The brushwork in later self-portraits is more expressive, and the color is more vibrant. It is no longer blended as in the early portrait but is broken up to create a richer texture and visual vibrancy.

◄ Self-Portrait with Grey Felt Hat *(1887–8). This self-portrait clearly shows how Vincent's brushwork became more dominant and expressive. The linear pattern created by the strokes puts greater emphasis on the eyes.*

Imprisoned

1890 Van Gogh exhibits in Brussels. Vincent's work is criticized by an artist who is then challenged to a duel by Toulouse-Lautrec. Favorable criticism of van Gogh's work by the critic Georges-Albert Aurier in the *Mercure de France* links it to the Symbolist artists. He is pleased that his work has received acclaim. Theo's son is born and named after Vincent, who is the child's godfather. Van Gogh dedicates *Blossoming Almond Tree* to his nephew. Van Gogh exhibits ten paintings at the Salon des Indépendants.

Vincent's fits became increasingly erratic and often occurred when he was working outdoors. In order to contain the problem, he was confined to working indoors by his doctors. He painted some of the views from the windows of the asylum and did some studies of the inmates. He also had to work from memory. This also gave him the chance to study the works of his favorite artists, such as Millet, Delacroix, and Rembrandt. He lacked the motivation to create new works and made over twenty copies of Millet's work. Vincent suffered a particularly bad attack, marked by his attempt to swallow paint. The paint was removed, and he was restricted to drawing.

▶ *Detail of* Old Man in Sorrow *(1890). Van Gogh has reworked one of his own drawings, but the peasant now resembles a fellow patient.*

▲ Prisoners Exercising *(1890). Rather than copying Doré's engraving accurately, van Gogh adjusted the colors to express his feelings about prison.*

A Prisoner

Vincent's confinement in the asylum was echoed in some of the works he created. His explanation of "not wanting to lose sight of the figure" as a reason for copying Millet's and Doré's works may have been true, but this does not explain his choice to create *Prisoners Exercising*. Van Gogh based this work on Doré's *The Prison Exercise Yard*, which depicts the monotonous life of the confined inmates.

Gustave Doré

Gustave Doré (1832–83) was one of the most successful illustrators and gifted caricaturists of the mid-nineteenth century. He showed the harsh reality of the working classes and also had a taste for the grotesque and the bizarre. He worked intermittently in London and earned a great deal of money. Vincent was a great admirer of Doré and of English engraving of this period.

▶ *Doré did 180 engravings for* London: A Pilgrimage, *including* Newgate – Exercise Yard *(1872), on which Vincent's* Prisoners Exercising *was based.*

▲ Noon: Rest from Work (after Millet) *(1890) is based on Millet's engraving. Although the subject matter connotes the idea of rest, the contrasting ochre and blue colors and the quivering brushwork create a strong nervous tension.*

▼ *Detail of* The Pietà *(1889). Some works painted during his time at Saint-Rémy show Vincent's return to his former interest in religion. He painted several biblical paintings like* The Pietà, *based on a Delacroix painting, and* The Raising of Lazarus, *based on a work by Rembrandt.*

▶ Harvesters Resting *(1850–53) by Millet depicts a biblical episode, but rather than setting this scene in the past, Millet set it in his contemporary world of peasant workers.*

Millet and Delacroix

Delacroix and Jean-François Millet (1814–75) were the two artists who inspired Vincent the most. Delacroix had rejected the academic approach of his predecessors and went off to North Africa inspired by the rich glowing colors of the Arab world. Vincent admired Delacroix's use of color. Millet, unlike Vincent, achieved recognition in his lifetime and even made some money, which afforded him a more comfortable lifestyle. Vincent mentions in his letters to Theo the high prices being paid for Millet's work. "It is enough to make you dizzy. So why think about it? — it would only daze our minds. Better to seek a little friendship and live from day to day. . . ." Clearly, Vincent did not aspire to a richer life.

Auvers-sur-Oise

1890 In February, *The Red Vineyard* sells in Brussels for 400 francs. Van Gogh rests for a month after another attack.
In May, Vincent visits Theo in Paris. Theo arranges for him to go to Auvers. He lives in the inn run by the Ravoux family. Dr. Gachet agrees to take care of him.
In July, Vincent visits Theo, who is preoccupied with business problems and his son's ill health. Van Gogh returns to Auvers.
On July 27, Vincent shoots himself.
On July 29, he dies at 1:30 a.m.
On July 30, he is buried in Auvers cemetery.

Theo moved his brother out of the asylum and found a sympathetic therapist, Dr. Gachet, in Auvers-sur-Oise to take care of him. Once settled, Vincent embarked on an intense period of work. He produced a number of panoramic landscapes. The wheatfields were particularly inspiring. Just weeks before his suicide, he wrote in a letter, "They are vast fields of wheat under troubled skies, and I did not need to go out of my way to try to express sadness and extreme loneliness. I hope you will see them soon . . . since I almost think that these canvases will tell you what I cannot say in words. . . ."

◀ Thatched Cottages *(1890). In Auvers-sur-Oise, Vincent was particularly attracted by the thatched roofs that he depicted with thickly laden brush strokes.*

▲ *Vincent died in this humble inn run by the Ravoux family.*

▼ The Church at Auvers *(1890). This is an accurate portrayal of the church at Auvers, but van Gogh has treated it as an organic form rather than as a static piece of architecture.*

Auvers-sur-Oise

Vincent found a room in a local inn but later rented a room in an inn owned by the Ravoux family. Vincent settled down to paint rural scenes showing the streets and cottages and countryside. It appeared that Vincent had settled into a happier, stable, and extremely productive period. He was fit enough during the summer to visit Theo in Paris and met up with his old friend Toulouse-Lautrec. Theo was preoccupied with the illness of his son and problems with his business, so Vincent returned to Auvers feeling like a greater burden than ever upon his brother.

Dr. Gachet

Dr. Gachet supported many contemporary artists. He was also an amateur painter, and Vincent "found a perfect friend in Dr. Gachet, something like a brother." Gachet encouraged Vincent to focus on his work rather than worrying about his illness, and Vincent produced more than eighty works in the few months he spent in Auvers. Like Vincent, Gachet suffered from depression. On his return from Paris, Vincent wrote to Theo of his concerns about Dr. Gachet, "In my opinion I don't think we can rely on Dr. Gachet at all. I just get the impression that he is more ill than myself, or, lets say, just as ill. If a blind man leads the blind, don't they both fall by the wayside?" Many questions were asked about the role Gachet played in Vincent's life. Some doubt whether he responded to Vincent's needs at all.

◀ Portrait of Dr. Gachet *(1890). This portrait sold for the highest amount ever paid for a painting at auction.*

The Final Curtain

Following his visit to Theo, when Theo warned him they would all have to tighten their belts, Vincent clearly felt insecure again. "My life" he wrote, "is also threatened at the very root, and my steps are also wavering." On the evening of July 27, armed with his equipment, he set out apparently to paint, but he had also packed a revolver. He shot himself in the chest but survived to stagger home and collapse in bed. Theo was summoned in time to spend time with his dying brother. Following Vincent's death, the local Catholic church refused to bury him because he had committed suicide. Instead, he was buried nearby at Méry on July 30. Many artists, along with his friends Pére Tanguy and Dr. Gachet, attended. His recent paintings were hung around the church, and his coffin was covered in yellow flowers.

The Goncourt Brothers

Vincent admired the work of the Goncourt brothers and demonstrated this by the inclusion of their books in his portrait of Dr. Gachet. Edmond (1822–96) and Jules (1830–70) produced articles on art criticism, social histories, and a series of naturalistic novels, including *Germinie Lacerteux* (1864) and *Madame Gervaisais* (1869).

▶ *Gauguin notes that the Goncourt brothers fueled Vincent's brain along with* The Bible.

▼ Wheat Field with Crows *(1890). Many believe that this painting conveys Vincent's own inner suffering and despair.*

Van Gogh's Legacy

Although Vincent had met with many of the established contemporary artists of his time, few regarded him as a great painter. "I can't change the fact that my paintings don't sell. But the time will come when people will recognize that they are worth more than the value of the paints used in the picture." This prediction of Vincent's proved correct. A group of his close companions, including Tanguy, Gauguin, Signac, Dr. Gachet, and especially Theo, had encouraged him, but none would have predicted the acclaim he is now given. His work was to influence the Fauves, the Expressionists, and others. During the last century, he rated among the most popular of artists. His life, letters, and works have been the subject of intense debate and analysis.

1890 Theo, with the help of Émile Bernard, holds a memorial exhibition of Vincent's paintings in his Paris apartment.
1891 Theo's health declines, and he dies on January 25. He is buried in Utrecht. His widow, Johanna van Gogh-Bonger, returns to the Netherlands with their infant son and Vincent's paintings.
1914 Joanna has Theo van Gogh's body exhumed and reburied in the Auvers cemetery next to Vincent.
1925 Johanna van Gogh-Bonger dies. Vincent Willem van Gogh inherits the collection of his uncle's paintings.
1962 Vincent Willem van Gogh transfers his collection to the Vincent van Gogh Foundation.
1969 Construction of the van Gogh Museum begins.
1973 The van Gogh Museum opens.

Vincent

▶ *Vincent's sister-in-law, seen here with her son Vincent Willem, was instrumental in establishing van Gogh's place in history.*

◀*Vincent signed some of his canvases with just his given name.*

▶ Self-Portrait in Front of the Easel *(1888).*

Becoming Famous

In 1891, Octave Mirbeau (1850–1917) wrote in his review of the Exhibition of the Indépendants that "I sense that I am in the presence of someone higher, more masterful, someone who disturbs me, moves me, and compels recognition." Georges-Albert Aurier (1865–92), the Symbolist poetry critic, applauded the "fire, intensity, and sunshine" of Vincent's work. Signac organized a posthumous exhibition at the Salon des Indépendants in 1891, and his ideas on art were exposed in the publication of some of his letters. Theo's widow, Johanna van Gogh-Bonger, returned to Holland, where she promoted Vincent's work. The Symbolist Jan Toorop (1858–1928), who had met Vincent in Paris, was a keen advocate of Vincent's work and introduced artists like Piet Mondrian (1872–1944) to his work. Vincent's use of color can be seen in the paintings Mondrian produced between 1907 and 1910. By 1894, his influence had spread to France, where artists like Édouard Vuillard (1868–1940), Pierre Bonnard (1867–1947), and other members of the Nabis group admired Vincent's work.

Van Gogh's Legacy

▼ Green Stripe *(1905) by Henri Matisse. The bold brush stroke of brilliant green defining Madame Matisse's brow heralded one of the most dramatic portraits of the time.*

The Fauves

By the turn of the twentieth century, the work of van Gogh, Gauguin, and Cézanne, with its fresh approach to color, was to encourage the next generation of young artists like Henri Matisse (1869–1954), Maurice de Vlaminck (1876–1958), Raoul Dufy (1877–1953), André Derain (1880–1954), and Georges Rouault (1871–1958). They rejected naturalistic color in favor of applying pure color to enhance the emotional force of the work in a rough, expressive style. The Impressionists had tried to capture light, whereas the Fauves used color to give their subjects a vibrant luminosity, much as Vincent had done. They changed the colors they saw to find the best color to express emotion. The Fauves were a loosely-associated group with Matisse as the dominant figure. They made a sensational impact in 1905 when they exhibited in the Salon d'Automne and again in 1906 at the Salon des Indépendants. The artists were labeled "wild beasts" for their bold, explorative approach, and the movement peaked at this point.

Die Brücke

Working in parallel to the Fauves, a group of German artists, among them Ernst Kirchner (1880–1938), Max Pechstein (1881–1955), and Emil Nolde (1867–1956), also sought to establish a new art. They called themselves Die Brücke. Kirchner formulated a manifesto to define their beliefs. Pechstein was to form links with the Fauves in Paris. Edvard Munch (1863–1944) and Ferdinand Hodler (1853–1918) were to influence a wilder Germanic style of Expressionism relating back to van Gogh, Gauguin, and the Fauves.

▲ *This painting,* Study for Portrait of van Gogh III *(1957) by Bacon, belongs to a group of eight paintings. It was based on Vincent van Gogh's self-portrait,* Painter on the Road to Tarascon.

Expressionists

The move away from recording a realistic view of the world, which Vincent had started, continued to develop. Vincent was regarded as "the Father of Expressionism." Artists looked inward to examine how they felt subjectively about their chosen themes and to give them spontaneous and dynamic responses. In order to strengthen this form of expression, they found it was necessary to take license with the accuracy of drawing form. In 1901, the first van Gogh exhibition in Germany was mounted. Later, the two Expressionist groups, Die Brücke and Der Blaue Reiter, took inspiration from van Gogh's works.

Francis Bacon

The philosophy of the twentieth-century British painter Francis Bacon (1909–92) that "Art is a method of opening up areas of feeling rather than merely an illustration of an object" was in line with van Gogh's own philosophy. Bacon dug deep into the darker side of the human psyche. He did a series of eight paintings based on van Gogh's *Painter on the Road to Tarascon*. In Bacon's interpretation, he converts the mood of optimism of the artist on the road into that of a lonely, tortured soul in line with his view of van Gogh. Bacon converts the shadow of the original painting into a threatening black form.

◀ The Scream *(1893), by the Norwegian artist Edvard Munch, is an icon of anguish and terror.*

Glossary

aesthetics The study, science, or philosophy of beauty.

authenticity The genuineness or legitimacy of something.

Baroque Of or related to the heavily ornamented style of European art of the seventeenth century.

capitalism A social or economic system based on the private ownership and trade of goods and services.

chiaroscuro An italian term meaning lightdark that describes an effect used in art, showing the contrast between light and shade.

commission The act of appointing someone to do a specific task, or the actual task given to someone under an agreement, especially in terms of creating a work of art.

composition The arrangement of the parts of something. The term is used to refer to the way in which objects are arranged, usually in a painting or sculpture.

cottage industry A small-scale business that can be run from home by family members using their own equipment.

delirium A usually brief state of mental agitation and confusion often accompanied by hallucinations.

epilepsy A mental disorder characterized by loss of consciousness and convulsions.

expressionism A movement in modern art that broke away from naturalism and distorted or exaggerated reality for emotional effect.

grotesque Having strange or unnatural qualities or proportions.

impasto A technique used in painting in which layers of paint are laid on the canvas, usually thickly enough that the brush or painting knife strokes can be seen. Paint is usually mixed right on the canvas.

impressionism A nineteenth-century art movement that took a more spontaneous approach to painting, attempting to capture and portray the atmosphere of a given moment, usually identified by a strong concern for the changing qualities of light.

Industrial Revolution The period of social and technological change that occurred in the eighteenth century, when agricultural nations became industrialized.

lithograph A print made by pressing paper onto a stone that has been engraved and treated with chemicals and water.

luminosity The quality of being luminous or emitting light; brightness.

manifesto A public statement made by a person or group, outlining their actions and intentions.

mass production The production of large quantities of manufactured goods by a standard process, for example, on production lines.

mentor A teacher; an experienced and trusted advisor or counsellor.

panorama A wide view of a scene, particularly a landscape.

philosophy The study of the nature and meaning of existence, reality, and knowledge. A set of rules or beliefs by which one lives.

picture plane The surface occupied by the foreground of a painting, from which perspective appears to recede.

pointillism A technique, also known as divisionism, used by Postimpressionists whereby a painting is made up of small dots of pure color that produce brilliant color effects when viewed from a distance.

Postimpressionism The term applied to a number of painters of the late nineteenth and early twentieth centuries whose style developed out of or in reaction against that of the Impressionists.

psyche The part of the mind responsible for one's thoughts and feelings.

realism In art, a movement that started in France in the mid-nineteenth century, the aim of which was to create accurate representations of reality.

retina The light-sensitive membrane covering the back of the eyeball that is connected to the optic nerve.

sacristan An officer of the church who is in charge of sacred objects.

sanatorium An hospital where people go to recover from or get treatment for chronic diseases.

schizophrenia A mental disorder in which a person's thoughts are disturbed, and he or she becomes detached from reality and withdraws from social contact.

socialism A political theory that advocates community ownership and control of the means of production, capital, land, and property and their administration and distribution in the interests of all.

symbolism A movement in art and literature that began in France in the 1880s and 1890s. It was a reaction against realism and sought to give visual expression to spiritual ideas through the use of color and lines.

tempera A kind of paint made when a pigment (colored fine powder) is mixed with water-soluble binding materials such as glue and egg yolk.

theology The study of religious beliefs and teachings.

Index

Index